09/05

$21.95

This book was donated
to honor
the birthday of

Katherine Harrs

by

Robert Hartford

2005

DATE

PRIMARY SOURCES IN AMERICAN HISTORY™

RECONSTRUCTION

A PRIMARY SOURCE HISTORY OF THE STRUGGLE TO UNITE THE NORTH AND SOUTH AFTER THE CIVIL WAR

TIMOTHY FLANAGAN

rosen central

Primary Source™

The Rosen Publishing Group, Inc., New York

In memory of Joseph Leo Flanagan II (1927–2002)

Published in 2005 by The Rosen Publishing Group, Inc.
29 East 21st Street, New York, NY 10010

Library of Congress Cataloging-in-Publication Data

Flanagan, Timothy.
Reconstruction: A primary source history of the struggle to unite the North and South after the Civil War/by Timothy Flanagan.
    p. cm.—(Primary sources in American history)
Summary: Uses primary source documents, narrative, and illustrations to recount the history of the Reconstruction, as the United States government and people worked to recover from the effects of the Civil War. Includes bibliographical references (p. 61) and index.
ISBN 1-4042-0177-7 (library binding)
1. Reconstruction—Juvenile literature. 2. Reconstruction—Sources—Juvenile literature. 3. United States—History—1865-1898—Juvenile literature. 4. United States—History—1865-1898—Sources—Juvenile literature. [1. Reconstruction. 2. Reconstruction—Sources. 3. African Americans—History—1863-1877—Sources. 4. United States—History—1865-1898. 5. United States—History—1865-1898—Sources.]
I. Title. II. Series: Primary sources in American history (New York, N.Y.)
E668.F57 2004
973.8—dc22

                                                                2003023338

Manufactured in the United States of America

On the front cover: *Bull Run, Virginia, Ruins of Mrs. Judith Henry's House.* Photograph taken by George Barnard in March 1862. Housed in the Library of Congress.

On the back cover: First row (left to right): John Bakken's sod house in Milton, North Dakota; Oswego Starch Factory in Oswego, New York. Second row (left to right): *American Progress,* painted by John Gast in 1872; the Battle of Palo Alto. Third row (left to right): Pony Express rider pursued by Native Americans on the plains; Union soldiers investigating the rubble of a Southern building.

ONTENTS

Introduction A Country Divided • **4**

Timeline • **8**

Chapter 1 Transition from War to Reconstruction • **10**

Chapter 2 Johnson v. the Radicals • **20**

Chapter 3 Radical Reconstruction • **30**

Chapter 4 The Struggle for Control • **39**

Chapter 5 Democrats Reclaim the South • **48**

Primary Source Transcriptions • **55**

Glossary • **57**

For More Information • **59**

For Further Reading • **60**

Bibliography • **61**

Primary Source Image List • **62**

Index • **63**

INTRODUCTION

A COUNTRY DIVIDED

In 1861, nearly ninety years after the United States was established, eleven Southern states decided to break free from the rest of the country. These states—Alabama, Arkansas, Florida, Georgia, Louisiana, Mississippi, North Carolina, South Carolina, Tennessee, Texas, and Virginia—set up their own country, which they called the Confederate States of America.

The principal reason for the secession, or separation, was slavery. All of the Confederate states were slave states, meaning that slavery was legal there. A great number of people in the nonslave states opposed slavery, and some were so strongly opposed that they formed groups to fight it. These people called themselves abolitionists.

Each state that makes up the United States of America has its own government, subject to the larger federal government under the U.S. Constitution. States can make their own laws as long as the laws do not violate the U.S. Constitution. Because the people in the slave states refused to stop buying and selling slaves, the federal government proposed an amendment to the Constitution that would abolish slavery everywhere in the United States.

People in the slave states were angry that the federal government was telling them what to do, which is why they decided to form their own country. That was not an acceptable solution as

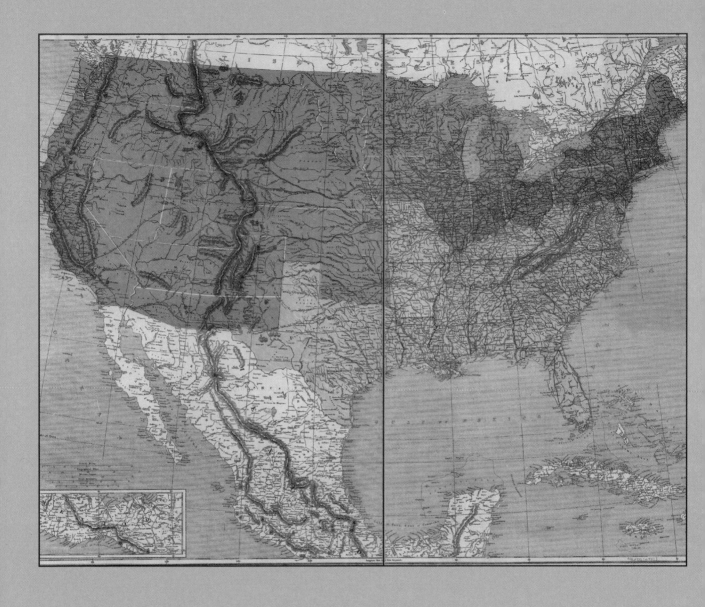

This 1861 map shows the United States after eleven Southern states had seceded from the Union. Note that the Confederate states (Alabama, Arkansas, Florida, Georgia, Louisiana, Mississippi, North Carolina, South Carolina, Tennessee, Texas, and Virginia) are shaded lighter than the rest of the country. The primary reason for the secession was the disagreement between the Southern states and the rest of the Union about the practice of slavery. Since the Confederate states refused to accept the Union's terms, the Civil War ensued.

far as the federal government and the rest of the country (called the Union) were concerned.

President Abraham Lincoln believed that slavery should end. He favored a gradual process, whereby the slave states would voluntarily free their slaves over a period of years, minimizing the chance for chaos. But the president's most important concern was keeping the country together. He was willing to find a compromise that would avoid bloodshed. In 1862, he wrote in a letter to Horace Greeley, a newspaper editor in New York, "If I could save the Union without freeing any slave I would do it, and if I could save it by freeing all the slaves I would do it; and if I could save it by freeing some and leaving others alone I would also do that."

Lincoln called his effort to bring the country together Reconstruction. In order for Reconstruction to succeed, all of the Confederate states had to be brought back into harmony with the Union. Since the Confederate states refused to compromise, they had to be taken by force. The Northern states formed an army called the Union army and fought the Southern states's Confederate army in the Civil War (1861–1865).

After the Union defeated the Confederacy, the president and Congress argued over the proper way to allow the Confederate states to rejoin the Union. There were major political, social, and economic factors at stake. Carl Schurz, a Union general who became a newspaper editor after the war, acknowledged the complicated situation in his Report on the Condition of the South, delivered to Congress and the president on December 19, 1865.

The war has not only defeated [Southerners'] political aspirations, but it has broken up their whole social organization. When the rebellion was put down they found themselves not only conquered in a political and military sense, but economically ruined.

The social and economic challenges of the Reconstruction were perhaps more painful and difficult for the country than the political aspects. In the same report, Schurz writes that the South's battle-scarred countryside

> looked for many miles like a broad black streak of ruin and desolation—the fences all gone; lonesome smoke stacks, surrounded by dark heaps of ashes and cinders, marking the spots where human habitation had stood; the fields along the road wildly overgrown by weeds, with here or there a sickly patch of cotton or corn cultivated by Negro squatters.

A true union of the North and South would take much more than a war victory. The entire country depended, at least in part, on the plantation system, which relied on slave labor. A change in that system would affect the economics of the North as well as the South. Political division, as well, made the unification process an angry one. The Confederate states were overwhelmingly loyal to the Democratic Party, while the Union states were aligned with the recently formed Republican Party.

Some Republicans wanted to keep the Southern states under strict military control and prevent them from rejoining the Union. Other, more moderate Republicans wanted to make it easy for the Southern states to rejoin the Union. The outcome of the power struggle among Republicans in Congress over the fate of the South had a permanent effect on the future of the United States.

TIMELINE

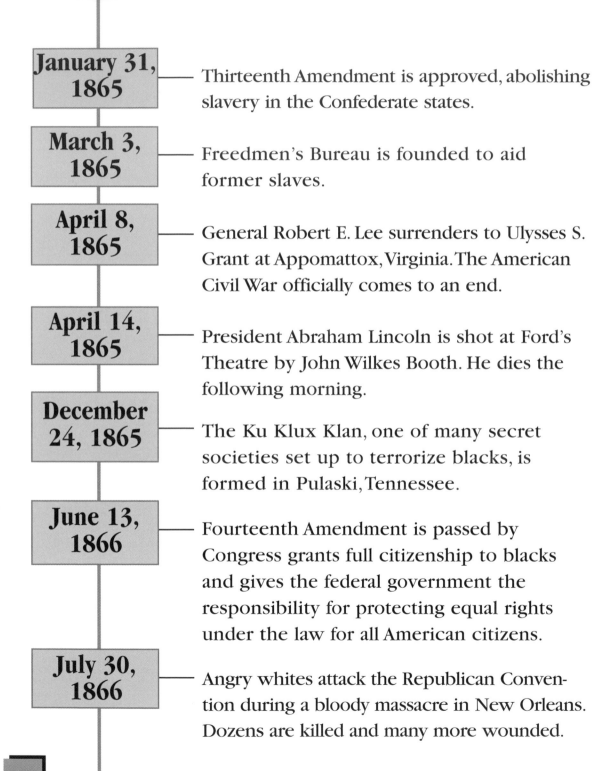

January 31, 1865 — Thirteenth Amendment is approved, abolishing slavery in the Confederate states.

March 3, 1865 — Freedmen's Bureau is founded to aid former slaves.

April 8, 1865 — General Robert E. Lee surrenders to Ulysses S. Grant at Appomattox, Virginia. The American Civil War officially comes to an end.

April 14, 1865 — President Abraham Lincoln is shot at Ford's Theatre by John Wilkes Booth. He dies the following morning.

December 24, 1865 — The Ku Klux Klan, one of many secret societies set up to terrorize blacks, is formed in Pulaski, Tennessee.

June 13, 1866 — Fourteenth Amendment is passed by Congress grants full citizenship to blacks and gives the federal government the responsibility for protecting equal rights under the law for all American citizens.

July 30, 1866 — Angry whites attack the Republican Convention during a bloody massacre in New Orleans. Dozens are killed and many more wounded.

TIMELINE

1867 — Three Reconstruction Acts defining Congress's new Reconstruction plan are passed.

1868 — Congress impeaches President Andrew Johnson, but he avoids conviction by one vote. Thaddeus Stevens dies, dimming the hopes of Radical Reconstruction.

1869 — Ulysses S. Grant is inaugurated president. Fifteenth Amendment is approved.

1871 — Ku Klux Klan Act is approved, allowing the federal government to act against terrorist organizations.

1872 — Congress abolishes Freedmen's Bureau, signaling decline of Radical Republican influence in Congress.

1875 — Civil Rights Act of 1875 is passed, asserting that all men are equal under the law.

1877 — President Rutherford B. Hayes removes last federal troops from South Carolina, officially ending Reconstruction.

CHAPTER 1

On April 8, 1865, after four years of fighting the Civil War, General Robert E. Lee of the Confederate army surrendered to General Ulysses S. Grant of the Union army at Appomattox Court House in Virginia. As a result of the war, the South was a ruined land, the slaves were free, and wealthy Southern landowners were nervous. How were they going to run their plantations without free slave labor? Would the freed slaves seek revenge? Would the Union army kick them off their farms? Even more uncertain, perhaps, were the newly freed slaves, for most of them lacked any sort of decent place to live. In the hearts and minds of many Southern whites, black people were less than human beings. At best, most Southern whites ignored the hardships of blacks; at worst, some tried to increase their suffering.

TRANSITION FROM WAR TO RECONSTRUCTION

The meeting of Grant and Lee is illustrated in this 1865 Currier and Ives lithograph, *Surrender of Genl Lee, at Appomattox C.H. Va April 9th 1865*, now housed in the Library of Congress. Appomattox Court House was the setting for the surrender of General Robert E. Lee, leader of the Confederate army, to Union general Ulysses S. Grant. This meeting marked the end of the Civil War and allowed Lincoln to begin his plan for Reconstruction.

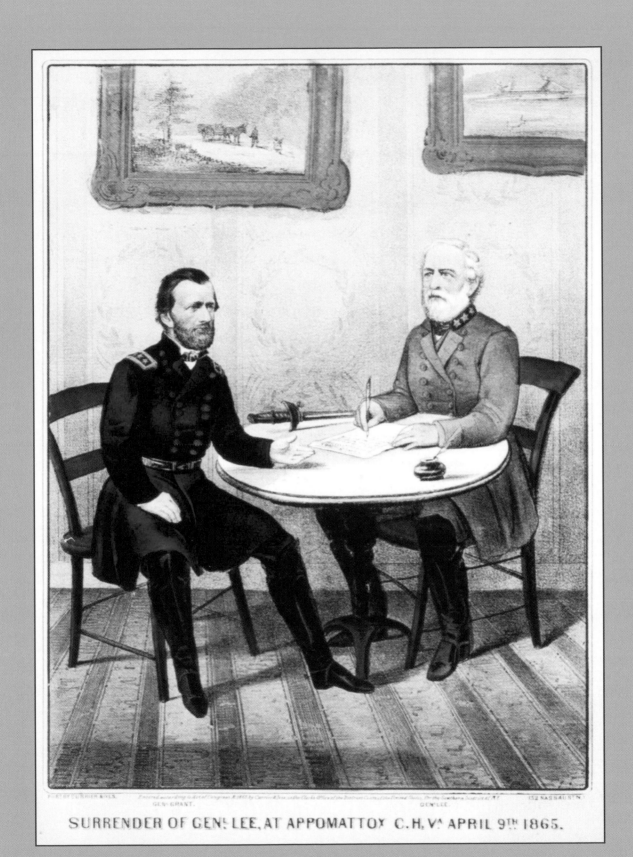

SURRENDER OF GEN^L LEE, AT APPOMATTOX C.H. V^A APRIL 9TH 1865.

As commander in chief, President Abraham Lincoln believed that it was his job alone to put the country back together. On March 4, 1865, in his second inaugural address, Lincoln spoke of his wish for a peaceful Reconstruction: "With malice toward none, with charity for all . . . let us strive on to finish the work we are in, to bind up the nation's wounds . . . to do all which may achieve and cherish a just and lasting peace."

Throughout the speech, Lincoln made it clear that he did not want to punish the South but rather bring the eleven Confederate states back into the Union as painlessly as possible. He proposed a lenient amnesty plan that would require one out of every ten men in a Confederate state to swear an oath of loyalty to the Union, in order for the state to be forgiven. At the same time, he recognized that the newly freed slaves had to be protected under the Thirteenth Amendment (1865), which stated, "Neither slavery nor involuntary servitude . . . shall exist within the United States."

The difference between an act and an amendment is important to know. An act is a law, and laws are only as good as the government's willingness to enforce them. But an amendment to the Constitution is a change in the agreement between the states and the federal government. When Congress passes an amendment to the Constitution, three-fourths of the states are required to agree to, or ratify, the amendment by a certain date. If enough states do not ratify the amendment, it does not become law.

The Thirteenth Amendment told Southerners that they would not be allowed back into the Union unless they accepted the freedom of the ex-slaves.

> by whom the offence came, shall we discern therein any departure from those divine attributes which the believers in a Living God always ascribe to Him? Fondly do we hope— fervently do we pray— that this mighty scourge of war may speedily pass away. Yet, if God wills that it continue, until all the wealth piled by the bond-man's two hundred and fifty years of unrequited toil shall be sunk, and until every drop of blood drawn with the lash, shall be paid by another drawn with the sword, as was said three thousand years ago, so still it must be said "the judgments of the Lord, are true and righteous altogether"
>
> With malice toward none; with charity for all; with firmness in the right, as God gives us to see the right, let us strive on to finish the work we are in; to bind up the nation's wounds; to care for him who shall have borne the battle, and for his widow, and his orphan— to do all which may achieve and cherish a just and a lasting peace, among ourselves, and with all nations.

Abraham Lincoln wrote his second inaugural address during the Civil War, which broke out just after he began his first term. No one had expected the war to last so long (four years) and to take as many lives (more than 600,000) as it did. Lincoln's address to the nation was dramatic and forceful, and he ended it with a passage begging for peace and unity, which was later carved into the walls of the Lincoln Memorial in Washington, D.C. See transcription excerpt on page 55.

Lincoln v. the Radical Republicans

Meanwhile, some members of Congress thought that Lincoln was too soft on the South for offering those states such an easy way of getting back into the Union. These senators and congressmen, all from the North and many of them deeply religious abolitionists, were known as the Radical Republicans. Led by Congressman Thaddeus Stevens of Pennsylvania and Senator Charles Sumner of Massachusetts, the Radical Republicans favored not only the abolition of slavery, but believed that freed slaves should have the same rights as white citizens, including the right to vote.

This indeed was a radical idea, because if the freed slaves were granted full citizenship and the right to vote, they would be able to build wealth and gain political power, thereby overthrowing the traditional social order of the South. The Radical Republicans looked forward to the total overthrow of the South as punishment for the Civil War. Speaking to the *New York Herald* after the war, Thaddeus Stevens said, "[Reconstruction] can only be done by treating and holding [white Southerners] as a conquered people. Then all things which we can desire to do follow with logical and legitimate authority."

In Stevens's opinion, the eleven Southern states should not be allowed to rejoin the Union, and the federal government should take total control of their lands. His religious views on the evils of slavery were at the core of his desire to punish and dominate the South. On January 3, 1867, Stevens addressed Congress: "What is Negro equality? It means . . . every man, no matter what his race or colour; every earthly being who has an immortal soul, has an equal right to justice, honesty, and fair play with every other man; and the law should secure him those rights."

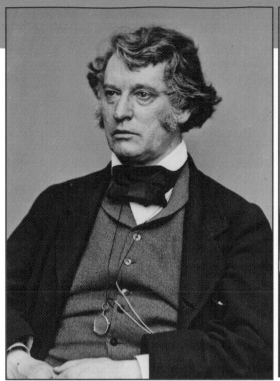

Radical Republican leaders Charles Sumner *(left)* and Thaddeus Stevens *(right)* worked tirelessly to get the country to accept their plan for Reconstruction. Sumner (1811–1874) is perhaps most famous for denouncing the Kansas-Nebraska Act, a piece of legislation that allowed the territories to decide whether they would allow slavery within their borders. An outraged congressman retaliated by attacking Sumner with a cane, a beating so brutal it took him three years to recover. At his own request, Stevens (1792–1868) was buried among African Americans in a Lancaster, Pennsylvania, cemetery. His gravestone explains his desire to be put to rest in the same way he lived his life, with "Equality of man before his Creator."

The conflict between President Lincoln and the Radical Republicans over Reconstruction policy was a battle over political power within the Republican Party. Lincoln himself was a Republican and, as president, was head of the Republican Party. Republicans had enjoyed nearly unchallenged power during the war because most Democrats had resigned from Congress and returned home to support the Confederacy. Now, Lincoln wanted to allow the Confederate states back into the Union and their Democratic representatives back into Congress. This would have allowed the Democratic Party to regain some measure of power. The Radical Republicans wanted to crush Southern Democrats, whom they viewed as traitors. Keeping the Southern Democrats out of Congress might have all but destroyed the Democratic Party.

The conflict between Lincoln and the Radical Republicans would never be resolved. On April 14, 1865, scarcely one month after his second inaugural address, President Abraham Lincoln was shot to death while attending a play at Ford's Theatre in Washington, D.C. The assassin was John Wilkes Booth, a popular actor and Confederate sympathizer from an established Northern family.

A New Administration

After Lincoln was assassinated, the Radical Republicans planned their political strategy. Vice President Andrew Johnson was suddenly president, and even though he was a Southern Democrat, the Radical Republicans believed he was agreeable to their cause—more agreeable, at least, than Lincoln had been.

The reason they believed this was that Johnson had been very vocal in his dislike for the wealthy Southern landowners who had controlled state and local governments in the South before the war. These relatively few landowners, sometimes called the planter class, had owned the vast majority of slaves. Members of the planter class had already lost much during the war (apart from their slaves), and the federal government's actions toward the South would determine whether they would lose more.

Before Lincoln was murdered, there was some hope among the planter class that they would keep their land. But now that Andrew

Published in *Frank Leslie's Illustrated Newspaper* on January 6, 1866, this illustration shows Andrew Johnson taking the presidential oath on April 15, 1865, after the assassination of Abraham Lincoln. Johnson (1808–1875) was raised in poverty by a single mother in North Carolina. Unschooled, he worked as a tailor and learned history from a man he hired to read to him while he worked. His humble beginnings and self-made qualities made him popular with the people, at least until he denounced the South's secession and supported the Union in the Civil War. That position got him onto Lincoln's reelection ticket as vice president, which led to his stepping in as president when Lincoln was shot.

Johnson was in charge, there was more than a little worry in the South that hard times were ahead. In a speech during his presidential campaign the year before, Johnson had used harsh words to describe the Confederates: "I say the traitor has ceased to be a citizen and in joining the rebellion has become a public enemy." To a group in Pennsylvania he proposed what should be done to the planters: "Their great plantations must be seized and divided into small farms, and sold to honest, industrious men."

Johnson's first move as president was to add restrictions to Lincoln's amnesty program. One of these restrictions prohibited wealthy Southern landowners from taking the loyalty oath and receiving amnesty. Even more severe, Johnson refused to grant Confederate military officers and wealthy landowners a general pardon that would restore their full citizenship. Initially, Radical Republicans were happy with Johnson's policy, even though he did not consult Congress officially before putting the plan into practice.

The Freedmen's Bureau

Although the Civil War had successfully freed slaves in the South, it also brought them much hardship. Most had nowhere to go once they left the plantations where they had lived. Few had food, money, or any of the basic necessities for life, and few Southerners were willing to help them. In response to these and other problems caused by the war, Congress established the Bureau of Refugees, Freedmen, and Abandoned Lands on March 3, 1865. The Freedmen's Bureau, as it was commonly known, was created to assist ex-slaves, called freedmen, with food, clothing, medicine, housing, and schooling.

The Freedmen's Bureau was supposed to function for only one year after the war, and in that year it did not have enough resources or power to serve the nearly 4 million ex-slaves. In February 1866, President Johnson vetoed a bill that would have extended the bureau's life and expanded its powers. This veto changed Radical Republicans' hopes for Johnson and marked the beginning of their bitter and unsuccessful battle with the president over Reconstruction. In July 1866, the Radicals had enough support in Congress from the moderate Republicans to override

A group of freed slaves poses for a photograph in Richmond, Virginia, in 1865. It wasn't enough to set slaves free after the Confederate states were defeated in the Civil War. Most freedmen were uneducated, had no money, and possessed no skills apart from those they used on the plantations or in the homes of their owners. The U.S. Bureau of Refugees, Freedmen, and Abandoned Lands (known as the Freedmen's Bureau) was created to provide freed slaves with basic necessities, medical care, and education.

Johnson's veto. They passed a bill to continue the Freedmen's Bureau and increase its power.

Debate over the Freedmen's Bureau clarified the two opposing positions regarding Reconstruction. Johnson and his supporters argued that the bureau was a war measure and should not exist during peacetime. The Radical Republicans did not consider the country to be at peace. Indeed, they considered most of the South to be in open defiance of the terms of their defeat, especially in their treatment of blacks. In their view, the war would not be over until the plantations were broken up and given to the ex-slaves. The Freedmen's Bureau, backed by military force, seemed the only means by which this victory could be achieved.

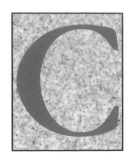

CHAPTER 2

JOHNSON V. THE RADICALS

Johnson sided with the elite Southern Democrats against the Radical Republicans because he saw them as the lesser of two evils. While he despised the big plantations of the South, he believed that the Republicans wanted to create Northern-style industrial cities in the South. When push came to shove, he thought that big industrial cities were worse than old-style Southern plantations.

By the end of 1865, every Southern state except Texas had elected a state government according to Johnson's amnesty rules. They also had elected new senators and representatives to Congress. Many of those elected were men who had not been allowed to vote according to the amnesty program. Johnson had left a loophole: The amnesty rules spoke only of citizenship and the right to vote, not the right to hold office. When Southerners elected men who were not qualified to receive amnesty, Johnson simply pardoned them using his powers as president. In his mind, Reconstruction was complete.

In these political cartoons, the unfair treatment toward blacks and Northerners during the Reconstruction era is satirized. At top, Justice is depicted as the snake-haired, mythological figure Medusa, weighing the scales in favor of the South. The two lower panels show examples of this "justice." At left, a Southern man is congratulated on murdering a black man. At right, a Northerner and a black man are lynched for murder.

When Congress returned to Washington in December of 1865, Johnson urged the Republicans to accept these new Southern senators and representatives, most of whom were Democrats. Instead, Congress rejected these new members, refusing to let them into their halls. They informed Johnson that his Reconstruction plan was unacceptable. Congress would accept new members under its terms, not the president's terms.

Congress rejected the new Southern "Johnsonian" governments for several reasons. The Republicans viewed most of the elected officials as traitors unworthy of Johnson's pardons. They saw the South's hostility to the Freedmen's Bureau and to blacks in general as a continuation of the war, and they were outraged by the new laws set up by Southern state and local governments to control the newly freed black population.

These laws, commonly known as the black codes, varied from state to state and county to county in their harshness. Their basic purpose was to keep blacks working on farms. Among other restrictions, blacks were not allowed to own land, work as free laborers, or serve as witnesses in court. Radical Republicans in Congress saw these codes as an attempt to reenslave blacks. During the first postwar year, the Freedmen's Bureau had only limited success in protecting ex-slaves from the abusive black codes. The Radical Republicans were determined to see the Freedmen's Bureau succeed.

The Joint Committee on Reconstruction

In December 1865, Congress had appointed a joint committee to look into conditions in the South. The committee gave its official report in April 1866. The news was not good: The South was in a state of confusion and civil disorder. In addition, the state

Thirty-ninth **Congress of the United States of America;**

At the *First* *Session,*

Begun and held at the City of Washington, on Monday, the *fourth* day of December, one thousand eight hundred and sixty-*five.*

AN ACT

To protect all persons in the United States in their civil rights, and furnish the means of their vindication.

Be it enacted by the Senate and House of Representatives of the United States of America in Congress assembled,

That all persons born in the United States and not subject to any foreign power, excluding Indians not taxed, are hereby declared to be citizens of the United States; and such citizens, of every race and color, without regard to any previous condition of slavery or involuntary servitude, except as a punishment for crime whereof the party shall have been duly convicted, shall have the same right, in every State and Territory in the United States, to make and enforce contracts, to sue, be parties and give evidence, to inherit, purchase, lease, sell, hold, and convey real and personal property, and to full and equal benefit of all laws and proceedings for the security of person and property, as is enjoyed by white citizens, and shall be subject to like punishment, pains, and penalties, and to none other, any law, statute, ordinance, regulation, or custom, to the contrary notwithstanding. Sec. 2. And be it further enacted, That any person who under color of any law, statute, ordinance, regulation, or custom, shall subject, or cause to be subjected, any inhabitant of any State or Territory to the deprivation of any right secured or protected by this act, or to different punishment, pains, or penalties on account of such person having at any time been held in a condition of slavery or involuntary servitude, except as a punishment for crime whereof the party shall have been duly convicted, or by reason of his color or race, than is prescribed for the punishment of white persons, shall be deemed guilty of a misdemeanor, and, on conviction, shall be punished by fine not exceeding one thousand dollars, or imprisonment not exceeding one year, or both, in the discretion of the court. Sec. 3. And be it further enacted, That the district courts of the United States, within their respective districts, shall have, exclusively of the courts of the several States, cognizance of all crimes and offences committed against the provisions of this act, and also, concurrently with the circuit courts of the United States, of all causes, civil and criminal, affecting persons who are denied or cannot enforce in the courts or judicial tribunals of the State or locality where they may be any of the rights secured to them by the first section of this act; and if any suit or prosecution, civil or criminal,

---

The Civil Rights Act of April 9, 1866, paved the way for the Fourteenth Amendment. This act granted citizenship to all persons born on American soil, including African Americans, who previously were denied citizenship. Although the Thirteenth Amendment had abolished slavery, the Civil Rights Act of 1866 specified the guarantee of certain rights for African Americans, such as the right to own property, enforce contracts, and give evidence in courts. See transcription excerpt on page 55.

governments of the South and Southerners in general were still hostile toward the United States. Armed with the evidence provided by the joint committee, Congress passed bills to increase the power of the Freedmen's Bureau and to guarantee more civil rights to blacks.

President Johnson had vetoed such bills the previous year, and this time was no different. On February 22, 1866, in a speech made to 6,000 Democratic admirers after he vetoed the Freedmen's Bureau Act and the Civil Rights Act (which declared that all persons born in the United States were now citizens, regardless of race), President Johnson proclaimed that the true enemies of Reconstruction were traitors in the North. People in the crowd called out for Johnson to name these traitors. He responded: "You ask me who they are? I say Thaddeus Stevens of Pennsylvania is one; I say Mr. Sumner of the Senate is another."

Johnson's personal attacks on the Radicals led moderate Republicans to side against Johnson and support the Radicals, even though they might not have agreed with their pro-black policies. In April 1866, Congress soon had enough votes to override President Johnson's vetoes of the Freedmen's Bureau Act and Civil Rights Act.

The Fourteenth Amendment

The Johnsonian governments of the South remained hostile to the Freedmen's Bureau and simply ignored the Civil Rights Act of 1866. Not only were blacks in the South not being given their civil rights as citizens, but many were being terrorized by vicious racists. Seeing that the Civil Rights Act and Freedmen's Bureau Act were not enough, Congress passed a new amendment to the Constitution in June 1866. The Fourteenth

The next step in Congress's Reconstruction plan was the Fourteenth Amendment, shown above, which was passed by Congress on June 13, 1866, and ratified on July 9, 1868. The document granted citizenship to "All persons born or naturalized in the United States," but that proved only half the battle. Enforcing the rights granted in the document was nearly impossible, and it would be years before the Fourteenth Amendment effectively changed the lives of African Americans. See transcription excerpt on page 56.

Amendment states that "all persons born in the United States of America . . . are citizens" and that "[no] State [shall] deprive any person of life, liberty, or property, without due process of law." Section 3 of the amendment stipulates that no public officials who had been involved in the rebellion could remain in office. This provision would make it possible for Congress to invalidate the Johnsonian governments in place in the South.

By passing the Fourteenth Amendment, Congress raised the stakes against the South. If any Southern states refused to ratify the amendment, they would never be readmitted to the Union and would be subject to Union military force once again. If they did pass the amendment, they would have to follow it to the letter or be subject to military force.

Unlike an act, an amendment does not require the signature of the president. In open hostility to Congress, Johnson spoke out publicly against the Fourteenth Amendment and urged the Southern states not to ratify it. Ten of the eleven Southern states took Johnson's advice and rejected the amendment.

Such political fighting threatened to tear the country apart again. The antiblack, racist messages put forth by the Democrats were answered loudly by the Republicans, who did their best to link the Democratic Party with treason and the Republican Party with patriotism.

In the 1866 congressional elections that followed, the Republicans won huge victories in federal and state elections. This united Congress had the power to override any veto Johnson might use against it. The result was that Congress could abolish the Johnsonian governments altogether and effectively start Reconstruction all over again, according to the Republicans' values.

Racial Violence

A small segment of the white population of the South held such deeply racist views of white superiority that they formed secret societies to commit violent acts against blacks and other groups that they considered enemies. The Ku Klux Klan (KKK) was the most widespread of these violent racist groups. Members of the KKK wore white sheets and white hoods when they carried out violent attacks on blacks. The sheets and hoods served two purposes: to keep people from knowing who they were and to strike fear in the hearts of their victims. The brutal terrorists on horseback covered in white from head to toe were supposed to be the ghosts of the Confederate soldiers killed during the war. These ghosts were said to be returning from the grave to seek revenge on the black man.

On July 30, 1866, twenty-five white elected officials in Louisiana, all Radical Republicans, met in New Orleans to draw up a new constitution that would get rid of the black codes and give blacks the right to vote. They were joined by 200 supporters, most of them black war veterans who had fought on the side of the Union. Fearing that Louisiana would no longer be under white control, a large number of former Confederate soldiers, aided by the New Orleans police, attacked the meeting. The delegates and their black supporters raised the white flag of surrender but were shot regardless as they tried to flee the building where the meeting was being held.

Federal troops were called in, but they arrived too late to stop the massacre. When it was over, more than 100 men were injured, and thirty-four blacks and three whites had been killed. What made the incident so horrific was that local police

The Ku Klux Klan began in 1866 in Pulaski, Tennessee, and was intended to be nothing more than a social club for Confederate veterans from the Civil War. But it soon became a secret organization fueled by hatred and racism, as members used violence to show their opposition to Radical Republicans. The two Klansmen in this illustration are shown in typical white hoods. Although its popularity varied throughout the years, with peaks in the late 1860s, 1920s, and 1960s, the goal of the Ku Klux Klan was always to achieve white supremacy in the United States.

participated in the attack, when it was their sworn duty to stop such crimes from happening. General P. H. Sheridan of the Union army investigated the incident, which was being called a race riot. On August 2, 1866, he wrote to Ulysses S. Grant, "The more information I obtain of the affair of the 30th in this city the more revolting it becomes. It was no riot; it was an absolute massacre—a murder perpetrated by the Mayor."

Another terrible incident occurred from May 1 through May 3, 1866, in Memphis, Tennessee, when a scuffle between a small group of black ex-Union soldiers and local whites turned into a two-day-long massacre of blacks in that city. The black population had grown so rapidly in Memphis after the war that whites were fearful of losing control. When a small fight broke out on the

This cover of the May 26, 1866, issue of *Harper's Weekly* features illustrations of two scenes from the Memphis riots. The top drawing shows a freedmen's school in flames, with a crowd of white rioters cheering at the sight. The illustration below depicts white men firing their rifles at blacks in what appears to be their town. Note the foreground images of slain bodies, pleading family members, and a man taking cover in a stream.

street, a group of black Union veterans who had been stationed there tried to stop it. Local whites overreacted. With the help of the police, they went around shooting as many blacks as they could find, women and children included. The massacre continued off and on for more than two days, and in the end, a large number of blacks had been injured and at least forty-six were killed. In contrast, two whites were killed.

There were many other smaller outbreaks of the same kind all over the South. Racial violence and secret terrorist groups like the KKK only showed the weakness of President Johnson's Reconstruction policies. If Congress had not acted to stop Johnson's policies, it is frightening to imagine how much worse life would have been for the supposedly free blacks in the South.

CHAPTER 3

RADICAL RECONSTRUCTION

It is important to stress that not all Democrats in the South hated blacks, but it is no surprise that the violent actions of a few, along with the lack of sympathy from many Southern whites, drove blacks to the Republican Party. Thaddeus Stevens and his fellow Radicals declared that they wanted to take land from rich plantation owners and give it to the freedmen to farm as their own. It seemed obvious to the Radicals that simply freeing slaves was not enough. Freedmen, they argued, needed education and economic advantages in order to fully participate in American life.

Forty Acres and a Mule

President Johnson opposed any form of land grants for blacks. Prior to 1866, small portions of land in Mississippi, Georgia, and South Carolina had already been given to freedmen to farm for their own profit. But Johnson used his presidential powers to give most of those farms back to their original owners. For example, the plantation of ex-Confederate president

Jefferson Davis had been confiscated during the war and given to seventy-five freedmen to farm. Johnson gave the plantation back to Davis and his brother.

Such actions enraged the Radicals. The always outspoken Thaddeus Stevens had made the position of the Radical Republicans perfectly clear in a speech before Congress in 1866. "The whole fabric of southern society must be changed," he proclaimed, "and never can it be done if this opportunity is lost." The debate over confiscation and land grants to ex-slaves raged in the North and in the South.

Blacks throughout the South continued to support the Republican Party. One reason was that Radical Republicans repeated the promise of "forty acres and a mule," which had made by General William T. Sherman during the Civil War when he entered Savannah, Georgia, on his fabled march to the sea. On January 16, 1865, General Sherman, with the support of Secretary of War Edwin M. Stanton, issued Special Field Order Number 15. This order, which was not a law, set aside the Sea Islands and a 30-mile (48-kilometer) inland tract of land along the southern coast of Charleston, South Carolina, for the exclusive settlement of blacks. Each family would receive 40 acres (16 hectares) of land and an army mule to work the land, thus "forty acres and a mule."

Even though Johnson returned to whites most of the land confiscated and given to blacks, the dream of "forty acres and a mule" was still very much in the minds of many ex-slaves. The Radical Republicans surely wanted to see that dream come true and, by repeating the promise, gained overwhelming support from blacks to the Republican Party.

General William Tecumseh Sherman (1820–1891) was one of the most successful Union leaders in the Civil War. He is most famous for his march to the sea, depicted above, on which he burned the city of Atlanta and destroyed much of the land of the South in order to disable the Confederacy. After the Civil War, Sherman was instrumental in "protecting" western lands from American Indians, using his position as general commander of the United States Army to force tribes to live on assigned reservations.

The Reconstruction Acts

Having gained solid control of both houses of Congress in the November elections of 1866, the Republicans set their own Reconstruction plan into motion. On March 2, 1867, Congress passed the Reconstruction Act over President Johnson's veto. Since Radical Republicans had failed to persuade enough of their colleagues to go along with any sort of land confiscation policy, the act did not provide former slaves with forty acres and a mule.

This kept blacks in a sort of middle space between slavery and freedom, for without an economic boost, most would have a very hard time rising out of poverty. In the end, lawmakers

40TH CONGRESS,
3D SESSION.

S. 662.

IN THE SENATE OF THE UNITED STATES.

DECEMBER 9, 1868.

Mr. SUMNER asked, and by unanimous consent obtained, leave to bring in the following bill; which was read twice and ordered to be printed.

A BILL

To carry out the reconstruction acts in the State of Georgia.

Whereas in the act of Congres entitled "An act for the more efficient government of the rebel States," among which is enumerated Georgia, it is provided that until the people of said rebel States shall by law be admitted to representation in Congress, any civil government which may exist therein shall be provisional only, and such States are divided into military districts; and whereas, in the supplementary reconstruction act bearing date July nineteenth, eighteen hundred and sixty-seven, it is further provided that "all persons hereafter elected or appointed to office in said military districts under any so-called State or municipal authority, shall be required to take and subscribe the oath of office prescribed by law for officers of the United States;" and whereas, it was the true intent and meaning of the act above mentioned that persons allowed to participate in the provisional legislation of any of the rebel States prior to their admission to representation by Congress, should take and subscribe the oath above mentioned; and whereas the legislature

Bill S. 662 of December 9, 1868, was intended to enforce the Reconstruction Acts in the state of Georgia. The bill ends with the words, "And be it further enacted, That the President be, and he is hereby, directed to place at the disposal of the provisional governor elect of Georgia, such portion of the army and navy of the United States as may be required by him for the preservation of the lives and property of persons, the peace and good order of the community, and the protection of citizens in the free expression of their political opinions." See transcription excerpt on page 56.

thought they could eventually give blacks the lift they needed through passing civil rights laws, but not by giving them land. They wanted change to take place slowly, thinking that the radical policies of Stevens and Sumner might cause more violence. Besides, they could find no clear wording in the U.S. Constitution that would allow them to confiscate land.

The Reconstruction Act outlined a plan to divide up the South (except Tennessee) into five districts. Each district was to be controlled by a general in the Union army. New elections were to be held in each state, with freed male slaves being allowed to vote. Congress would allow the Southern states to be readmitted to the Union after they agreed to enforce the Fourteenth Amendment and to guarantee the black vote. Two hundred thousand Union troops were brought in to prevent any major violence and to make sure the people in the South did not try to stop blacks from voting.

The Fourteenth Amendment and the Reconstruction Act effectively invalidated the black codes. Though the racist attitudes that gave rise to the black codes remained, for the time being the codes were no longer in force in most places in the South.

In the weeks that followed, Congress passed two additional acts to strengthen the Reconstruction Act. This was necessary because President Johnson kept trying to stop enforcement and because the Southern states themselves resisted. The Second Reconstruction Act, passed on March 23, 1867, authorized military commanders to supervise elections and spelled out the rules the Southern states had to follow in setting up new state governments. The Third Reconstruction Act, passed on July 19, 1867, reminded the South that it was under strict military control and would remain so until it followed the

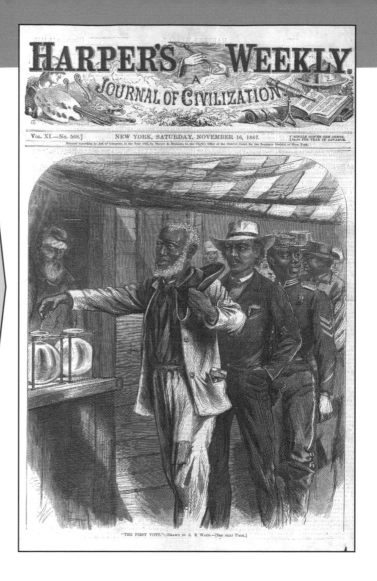

HARPER'S WEEKLY.

A

JOURNAL OF CIVILIZATION

VOL. XI.—No. 568.] NEW YORK, SATURDAY, NOVEMBER 16, 1867. [SINGLE COPIES TEN CENTS.
[$4.00 PER YEAR IN ADVANCE.

"THE FIRST VOTE."—DRAWN BY A. R. WAUD.—[SEE NEXT PAGE.]

The First Vote, an illustration from the November 16, 1867, issue of *Harper's Weekly* depicts African American men lined up to vote. The magazine noted, "The freedmen are represented marching to the ballot-box to deposit their first vote, not with expressions of exultation or of defiance of their old masters and present opponents depicted on their countenances, but looking serious and solemn and determined."

rules. The difference between the Reconstruction Acts and the Civil Rights Act was that the Reconstruction Acts were backed up by military troops. Memories of the horrors of war were very real in the minds of Southerners, and the presence of soldiers was the only thing that could change their behavior toward ex-slaves.

The Union military commanders were given the job of carrying out the Reconstruction program. The process moved forward one step at a time. The commanders were to enroll qualified voters, including blacks and excluding whites barred from holding office by the Fourteenth Amendment. Then they were to hold elections for new state conventions. Each state convention was to write a new constitution that guaranteed blacks the right to vote. Once the constitution was agreed to by a popular vote, a state governor and body of lawmakers could be elected. These lawmakers then had to ratify the Fourteenth Amendment. Finally, Congress had to approve of the new state constitution before the state would be allowed to send elected representatives to Congress.

Johnson Impeached

The Reconstruction Acts so angered President Johnson that he attempted to fire the secretary of war, Edwin Stanton. Stanton had approved General Sherman's "forty acres and a mule" order. The president knew that Stanton, though a Democrat, would use his power to aggressively enforce the Reconstruction Acts.

Johnson wanted to appoint retired general Ulysses S. Grant, the commander of the victorious Union army, to replace Stanton as secretary of war. The president believed he could control Grant and keep him from enforcing the Reconstruction Acts. It was clear that Johnson was prepared to do just about anything to have his own way. When he announced the dismissal of Stanton and the appointment of Grant, Grant flatly refused. The battle-worn general wanted nothing to do with Johnson's scheme and made it known that he was on the side of the Radicals.

Some of Johnson's friends urged him to use the military to stop Congress from meeting. Luckily, the president was not willing to go that far, for that could have spelled the end of the United States. Still, attempting to fire a cabinet member approved by the Senate without good cause was seen as a violation of the law, and Congress was determined to punish Johnson by impeachment.

Secretary of War Edwin M. Stanton (1814–1869) came into power during President Lincoln's administration. After Lincoln's assassination, Stanton essentially ran the government until Andrew Johnson took over the presidency. At odds with Johnson's position on Reconstruction, Stanton secretly represented the Radical Republicans in the presidential cabinet. Johnson's attempts to fire Stanton resulted in his impeachment. But when Johnson stayed in office, Stanton was forced to resign.

In the end, Johnson's enemies fell one vote short of removing him from office, but the impeachment process was the final blow to the president's Reconstruction policies. For example, Congress continued to support the Freedmen's Bureau and the good work it did for blacks. Johnson had been against the Freedmen's Bureau, but after the impeachment he lacked the support to interfere with its work.

Congress was running Reconstruction now, but the Radical Republicans were still not the majority. It was true that the vast black population had a better chance of enjoying freedom now that President Johnson (and his fellow Democrats) had been stripped of power and the black codes had been abolished, but

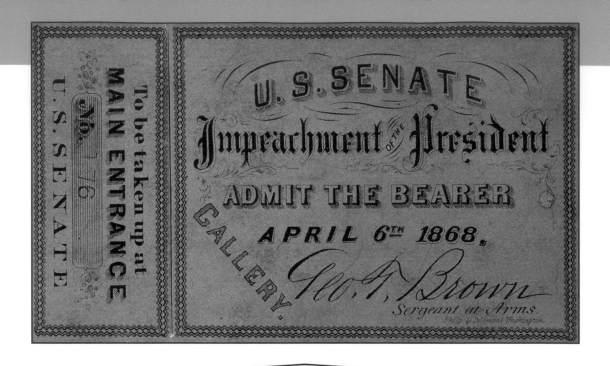

U.S. SENATE

To be taken up at
MAIN ENTRANCE

No. 176

U.S. SENATE

U.S. SENATE

Impeachment of the President

ADMIT THE BEARER

APRIL 6TH 1868.

Geo. T. Brown

Sergeant-at-Arms.

GALLERY.

Tickets such as this one were printed for President Andrew Johnson's impeachment trial. Johnson was the first U.S. president to be impeached, and the situation created much excitement and anxiety in the country. People worried that if Congress had the power to remove a president from office, then the country risked being turned into a dictatorship. Throughout U.S. history, however, only three presidents have been impeached: Johnson in 1868, Bill Clinton in 1998, and Richard Nixon, who resigned in 1974 during the impeachment process.

the fact remained that the Radical Republican vision of true racial equality was not going to happen anytime soon.

In the presidential election of 1868, Ulysses S. Grant was elected president. Andrew Johnson went back to Tennessee and died a few years later, a bitter and defeated man.

CHAPTER 4

The people of the South had no choice but to follow the rules spelled out by Congress. If they refused, they would remain under military control. So they held elections. But—since whites still were the majority in the South—naturally, white candidates won most of the elections. Of course racism was a major factor in elections, but education also came into play. Very few blacks could read or write, and it was unthinkable for an illiterate person to run for an elected office.

THE STRUGGLE FOR CONTROL

Notable Black Leaders

One former slave who could read and write was Oscar J. Dunn. The people of Louisiana elected him to the office of lieutenant governor. It was the highest executive office held by a freedmen to date. Dunn had run away from slavery prior to the war, a crime sometimes punished by death to make other slaves think twice about doing the same thing. He managed to begin his education before slavery ended, which was a rare thing indeed. Very few slaveholders taught their slaves how to read and write, and otherwise it was nearly impossible for slaves to become educated. While it is true that not all blacks in the South had been slaves (some free blacks had actually fought for the Confederacy), the number of educated free blacks was quite small. During Reconstruction, black men with an education were encouraged to run for office. Dunn served as fine example to both blacks and whites, for he was determined, courageous, and honest.

Francis L. Cardozo graduated from the University of Glasgow in Scotland and was a church minister in Connecticut at the time of the Civil War. After the war, he returned to his native South Carolina to run a school for blacks. In 1868, he was elected secretary of state in South Carolina and served until 1872. Speaking to the state's lawmakers in 1868 about the need to get blacks off the farms and into schools, Cardozo said: "We will never have true freedom until we abolish the system of agriculture which existed in the Southern states. It is useless to have any schools while we maintain the stronghold of slavery as the agricultural system of the country."

Such a position put Cardozo on the same side as Thaddeus Stevens and the Radical Republicans, who still had some influence in Congress. But on August 11, 1868, Thaddeus Stevens died. He had been one of the great supporters of fair treatment of blacks, and with his death the dream of breaking up the plantations began to fade. While there were other able and passionate advocates for black people, Stevens had been a true champion and there was no one who could fill his shoes.

John W. Menard from Louisiana was the first black elected to Congress. The Louisiana Congress did not admit Menard, choosing to leave his seat empty. Racial prejudice was deep, and even though Congress outwardly professed a desire for blacks to have equal rights, its true feelings about race became clear when it chose to keep a black politician out of its halls.

This 1869 wood engraving, an illustration from *Frank Leslie's Illustrated Newspaper*, shows John Menard addressing the House of Representatives on February 27, 1869. Though held back in many ways because of the color of his skin, Menard (1838–1893) managed to influence U.S. history, most notably as a newspaper publisher.

Carpetbaggers and Scalawags

In the Radical Reconstruction years, the number of blacks present in the new state governments had a lot to do with the presence of carpetbaggers and scalawags in the state. Some Northerners came to the South to take advantage of the confusion during the tough Reconstruction years, carrying their belongings from place to place in carpetbags, large traveling bags made of carpet. Southerners called these Northerners carpetbaggers, and it was

No matter what their purpose, Northerners who went to the South after the Civil War were not looked upon kindly. In this political cartoon from *Harper's Weekly*, illustrator Thomas Nast criticizes Carl Schurz (1829–1906), a liberal Republican, by portraying him as a carpetbagger sympathetic to the post-war South.

not said kindly. As time went on, the term came to mean any Northerner who came to the South to meddle in Southern affairs. While it is true that some Northerners went to the South for purely selfish motives (either for money, political power, or both), most of the so-called carpetbaggers were there for honest reasons. Some went to set up much-needed businesses. Some went to help build the railroad. Others went to set up schools for blacks and poor whites, to build churches, and to help the Freedmen's Bureau hand out clothing and medical supplies.

Southerners treated nearly all of the Northern invaders, whether honest or dishonest, with hostility. The most hated Northerners were the ones who became active in Radical politics and in organizing the black vote. Nothing was more threatening to the average white Southerner than a black man with a ballot, because ex-slaves could thus change society for their betterment.

Some white Southerners, however, did not feel threatened by the changes taking place in their society. Some had the courage to help the Northerners. They were called scalawags by those who hated what they were doing. The word "scalawag" means troublemaker, but when one Southerner called another a scalawag it carried a much greater sense of condemnation.

In cartoons, scalawags were pictured as low-down, dirty people, the scum of the earth. But in reality, more than a few note-worthy people joined the cause of the Radical Republicans. Lieutenant General James A. Longstreet of the Confederate army, one of General Lee's most able commanders, accepted defeat and became a Republican. James L. Orr, an outspoken rebel before the war and a Confederate senator, backed the Radicals in 1868. Orr became the first postwar governor of South Carolina and worked to pass some limited civil rights legislation. Wealthy Mississippi slaveholder R. W. Flournoy joined the Radicals not out of greed but out of sympathy for the ex-slaves. After the war, he corre-sponded with Thaddeus Stevens and expressed his willingness to help. Because of his support for racial equality, Flournoy was the most hated man in Mississippi.

Certainly, Longstreet, Orr, and Flournoy did not fit the mold of a vile scalawag. But there were plenty who did—men without any feeling for slaves, men who sided with Republicans in the hopes of making money. In the South there were many poor whites who, like the Northern Republicans, disliked the planter class and wanted to see it broken. Some of these people were able to put aside their racial prejudice and side

Francis Cardozo *(left)* and James Orr *(right)* are shown in the photographs above. Cardozo (1837–1903) is best known as the first African American to hold a government office in South Carolina. He was born free in the South and was educated in Scotland and England. He returned to the United States as a minister before he became involved in politics. Orr (1822–1873) was the first South Carolina governor elected by popular vote. He also served in the U.S. Congress and as the U.S. minister to Russia. Orr is an example of a so-called scalawag who worked hard to rebuild the South.

with the Republicans, thinking that they would share in the free land if the plantations were broken up. There were many different reasons why men became scalawags, though the racist, Southern white Democrats did not trouble themselves with such fine distinctions.

Where there were a large black population and a large number of carpetbaggers and scalawags, more blacks were elected to state and local offices. In South Carolina, Louisiana, Virginia, and Florida, blacks won a lot of elections and were seen as a real threat to white rule. In North Carolina, Texas, and Arkansas, whites remained firmly in control. Alabama, Georgia, and Mississippi were somewhere in between.

In 1868, Congress voted to readmit seven states to the Union: Alabama, Arkansas, Florida, Georgia, Louisiana, North Carolina, and South Carolina. Soon after, as though to test the will of the federal government, Georgia expelled its twenty-six elected black state representatives. Clearly, this was illegal. Congress reimposed military rule over Georgia. Eventually, Georgia agreed to let the black representatives back in and was then admitted to the Union.

The Fifteenth Amendment

In 1869 and 1870, Southern states began replacing the Republican state governments (which included blacks) that had been more or less forced on them by Congress. They elected all-white Democratic state governments, called redeemer governments, because they redeemed white control. Other factors that helped the Democrats to gradually "redeem" the South were the lack of education of most blacks and the sometimes outrageous political and financial corruption of carpetbaggers, which caused many Southern Republicans to vote against them.

The redeemer governments often were controlled by the planters who had dominated Southern politics before the Civil War, and these governments did their best to keep blacks poor and uneducated so as to keep them from voting in large numbers. There was so much prejudice against blacks that Congress saw the need to propose the Fifteenth Amendment to make it perfectly

Fortieth Congress of the United States of America;

At the *third* Session,

Begun and held at the city of Washington, on Monday, the *seventh* day of *December*, one thousand eight hundred and *sixty-eight*.

A RESOLUTION

Proposing an amendment to the Constitution of the United States.

Resolved by the Senate and House of Representatives of the United States of America in Congress assembled,

(two-thirds of both Houses concurring) That the following article be proposed to the legislatures of the several States as an amendment to the Constitution of the United States, which, when ratified by three-fourths of said legislatures shall be valid as part of the Constitution, namely:

Article XV.

Section 1. The right of citizens of the United States to vote shall not be denied or abridged by the United States or by any State on account of race, color, or previous condition of servitude—

Section 2. The Congress shall have power to enforce this article by appropriate legislation—

Schuyler Colfax
Speaker of the House of Representatives.

B. F. Wade
President of the Senate pro tempore.

Attest:
Edward McPherson
Clerk of House of Representatives.

Geo. C. Gorham
Secy of Senate U.S.

The Fifteenth Amendment was passed by Congress on February 26, 1869, and ratified on February 3, 1870. The amendment gave black males the right to vote, but, like the Thirteenth and Fourteenth Amendments, it was largely ignored in practice. Finally, in 1965, President Lyndon B. Johnson asked Congress to pass legislation that would make ignoring the Fifteenth Amendment illegal, saying, "we cannot have government for all the people until we first make certain it is government of and by all the people." See transcription excerpt of the amendment on page 56.

clear to the South that blacks could not be denied the right to vote. The Fourteenth Amendment and the several Reconstruction Acts had not been quite strong enough in their wording about black voting, called suffrage. The Fifteenth Amendment, which stated that the right to vote could not "be denied . . . on account of race, color, or previous condition of servitude," was a direct response to Southern hostility to the black vote.

But the hostility did not end. The white redeemer governments were not enforcing the laws designed to protect blacks. So in 1870, Congress passed the Enforcement Act to give the federal government the power to deal with whites who attempted to stop blacks from voting. In 1871, with the support of President Grant, Congress passed a second enforcement act called the Ku Klux Klan Act. This act specifically targeted the KKK and similar white supremacist terrorist groups.

Unfortunately, as Republicans began to lose power in the South, these acts became more and more difficult to enforce, and blacks continued to suffer greatly. By 1872, Radical Republicans did not have enough power to keep the Freedmen's Bureau going, and Congress voted to abolish it.

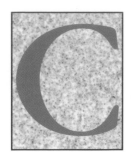

CHAPTER 5

DEMOCRATS RECLAIM THE SOUTH

President Ulysses S. Grant was not a very strong leader when it came to Reconstruction. The country needed a firm hand in this period of social change, and Grant failed to provide it. He allowed Congress to drive the policies and did not get in its way. Since the Radical Republicans did not have a majority in Congress, there was little they could do to help blacks and poor whites in the South. In the early 1870s, Democrats regained more and more power in Southern states. One reason was the deaths of prominent Radicals, namely Thaddeus Stevens and Charles Sumner. As the Radical push of social and economic reform continued to weaken, the less well-meaning Republicans used their power to promote business opportunities for themselves and other Northerners. The issue of racial equality took a back seat to economic expansion.

The Panic of 1873 brought chaos to Wall Street, as shown in this illustration from the October 11, 1873, issue of *Harper's Weekly.* This major financial disturbance began when railroads and other American businesses realized they had overextended themselves during a financial boom and were forced into bankruptcy, creating an economic crisis in the United States that led to a depression. A focus on these economic hardships meant that many Reconstruction issues were put on the back burner, and blacks in the South were greatly affected.

RUN ON THE UNION TRUST COMPANY.

But business and industry suffered a major setback with what became known as the Panic of 1873. For a series of complex reasons, a lot of people who had invested in new businesses lost their money, and the economic boom came to a halt. This is known as a depression. The Panic of 1873 caused a depression that lasted about four years. People blamed President Grant and the Republicans for letting businessmen do whatever they wanted without any government oversight. Workers were fed up with the poor treatment they received. Such tensions further weakened the Republican Party, and many workers switched to the Democratic Party.

In 1873, Texas fell to the Democrats and its citizens elected an all-white redeemer government. In 1874, for the first time since before the Civil War, Democrats won control of Congress. The Democrats were on their way to creating a so-called solid South, meaning a South controlled solely by Democrats with no blacks in government. If they could accomplish this, they thought, the South would be redeemed and they could keep blacks "in their place" forever.

Republican Scandals Help the Democrats

The Republican Party continued to suffer from scandals involving its own officials. These scandals typically involved theft of taxpayer monies. The worst of these came in 1875 and involved the Whiskey Ring, a criminal organization centered in St. Louis, Missouri, that stretched into every major city in the country. This ring of government employees, liquor makers, store owners, newspaper men, and others stole millions in liquor taxes that were supposed to go to the federal government. Hundreds of men were arrested, and the scandal seriously damaged the

This 1876 cartoon by Thomas Nast is called *In for It*. Nast depicts Secretary of War William Belknap diving into a barrel of corruption, saying "I hope I shall get to the bottom soon." The rings of the barrel are labeled with names of the many U.S. scandals that took place during Ulysses Grant's administration, including the Tammany (Hall) Ring, the Canal Ring, and the Whiskey Ring. Belknap was impeached for accepting bribes from companies who wanted to trade on Native American reservations (the Indian Ring). Because of all of the scandals during this time, the term "Grantism" was coined, meant to invoke notions of greed and corruption.

IN FOR IT.
U. S. "I hope I shall get to the bottom soon."

reputation of the Republican Party. There was a lot of fighting within the party, and this lack of unity made it hard for Republicans to promote their causes.

Meanwhile, the Democrats were united by a single goal: to reclaim the South. White supremacist groups became more active. In Mississippi, organized bands used force to prevent blacks from voting. Many black people were beaten and killed under what was known as the Mississippi Plan. White Democrats in other states began using the Mississippi Plan to strike fear in blacks and keep them from voting. Sometimes, blacks were held at gunpoint and forced to vote for the Democratic candidates. Other times, they were told they would lose their jobs if they voted.

Most blacks considered themselves Republicans, but when they saw that Republicans in Washington were not interested in defending them against cruel treatment at the hands of white Democrats, they rejected "the Party of Lincoln." By 1876, only Florida, South Carolina, and Louisiana were still controlled by the Republicans.

Throughout the South, whites and blacks were largely separated in public life. Blacks were barred from white-owned restaurants, inns, and other public establishments. White and black children attended separate schools, and the white schools were generally better staffed and better funded. This forced separation of the races was known as segregation. Though segregation seemed to go against the spirit of the Fourteenth Amendment, most whites and many blacks accepted it as the natural order of things.

An Incomplete Reconstruction

A new Republican president, Rutherford B. Hayes, took office in 1876 in a hotly disputed election. In a speech made shortly after Hayes took office, Republican governor Daniel Henry Chamberlain of South Carolina asked, "What is the President's Southern Policy?" Then he answered his own question: "[I]t consists of the abandonment of Southern Republicans, and especially of the colored race, not only to control and rule of the Democratic Party, but of the class at the South which regarded slavery as a Divine Institution."

In 1877, Hayes withdrew the last remaining federal troops from the South. This officially marked the end of the Reconstruction era, but it was an incomplete Reconstruction. It would not take long for Democrats to achieve their goal of a solid South. While the Confederate states had technically been

THE "STRONG" GOVERNMENT 1869–1877.   THE "WEAK" GOVERNMENT 1877–1881.

Illustrated by James Albert Wales and printed in the May 12, 1880, issue of *Puck*, this two-part cartoon is titled, *The "Strong" Government 1869–1877— The "Weak" Government 1877–1881*. The panel on the left shows a woman (labeled "the Solid South") carrying a carpetbag containing Ulysses S. Grant. The bag is marked, "carpet bag and bayonet rule." The panel on the right shows Rutherford B. Hayes plowing over the carpetbag and bayonets. His plow is marked, "Let 'em alone policy." The cartoon compares the high hopes of Grant's Reconstruction plan with Hayes's virtual abandonment of the issue.

reunited with the Union, the basic way of life in the South had not been radically changed, in so far as whites still dominated the black population. It was not enough for the Republicans to pass the Thirteenth, Fourteenth, and Fifteenth Amendments. Clearly, white Southerners had no interest in following the law with regard to blacks, and in the end the Republican Party was not united in its duty to make sure that the South obeyed the federal law.

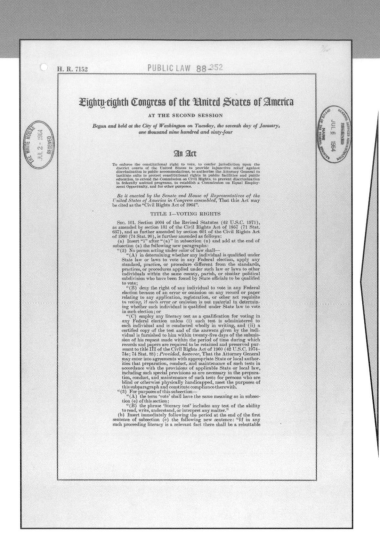

The Civil Rights Act of 1964 was inspired by President John F. Kennedy and was signed into law by his successor, Lyndon B. Johnson. The act banned most segregation and discrimination practices in the United States. It had taken nearly a century for the U.S. government to pass and enforce legislation that reflected Abraham Lincoln's original Reconstruction plan. See transcription excerpt on page 56.

The vision shared by Stevens, Sumner, and a host of other good-hearted Radical leaders was not achieved, but at least the proper laws were in place. However, it would take decades before blacks, Native Americans, and women would begin to enjoy some measure of fair treatment under the law. The Civil Rights Acts of 1963 and 1964, passed by a Republican-controlled Congress, were the last federal laws to outlaw race discrimination. Even then, nearly ninety years after the Civil War ended, Reconstruction was still going on.

PRIMARY SOURCE TRANSCRIPTIONS

Page 13: President Lincoln's second inaugural address

Transcription excerpt

Fellow Countrymen:

On the occasion corresponding to this four years ago, all thoughts were anxiously directed to an impending civil-war. All dreaded it—all sought to avert it. While the inaugural address was being delivered from this place, devoted altogether to saving the Union without war, insurgent agents were in the city seeking to destroy it without war—seeking to dissolve the Union, and divide effects, by negotiation. Both parties deprecated war; but one of them would make war rather than let the nation survive; and the other would accept war rather than let it perish. And the war came.

Fondly do we hope—fervently do we pray—that this mighty scourge of war may speedily pass away. Yet, if God wills that it continue, until all the wealth piled by the bond-man's two hundred and fifty years of unrequited toil shall be sunk, and until every drop of blood drawn with the lash, shall be paid by another drawn with the sword, as was said three thousand years ago, so still it must be said "the judgments of the Lord, are true and righteous altogether."

Page 23: Civil Rights Act of 1866

Transcription excerpt

An Act to protect all Persons in the United States in their Civil Rights, and furnish the Means of their Vindication.

Be it enacted by the Senate and House of Representatives of the United States of America in Congress assembled, That all persons born in the United States and not subject to any foreign power, excluding Indians not taxed, are hereby declared to be citizens of the United States; and such citizens, of every race and color, without regard to any previous condition of slavery or involuntary servitude, except as a punishment for crime whereof the party shall have been duly convicted, shall have the same right, in every State and Territory in the United States, to make and enforce contracts, to sue, be parties, and give evidence, to inherit, purchase, lease, sell, hold, and convey real and personal property, and to full and equal benefit of all laws and proceedings for the security of person and property, as is enjoyed by white citizens, and shall be subject to like punishment, pains, and penalties, and to none other, any law, statute, ordinance, regulation, or custom, to the contrary notwithstanding.

Sec. 2. And be it further enacted, That any person who, under color of any law, statute, ordinance, regulation, or custom, shall subject, or cause to be subjected, any inhabitant of any State or Territory to the deprivation of any right secured or protected by this act, or to different punishment, pains, or penalties on account of such person having at any time been held in a condition of slavery or involuntary servitude, except as a punishment for crime whereof the party shall have been duly convicted, or by reason of his color or race, than is prescribed for the punishment of white persons, shall be deemed guilty of a misdemeanor, and, on conviction, shall be punished by fine not exceeding one thousand dollars, or imprisonment not exceeding one year, or both, in the discretion of the court.

Page 25: Fourteenth Amendment to the U.S. Constitution

Transcription excerpt

All persons born or naturalized in the United States, and subject to the jurisdiction thereof, are citizens of the United States and of the State wherein they reside. No State shall make or enforce any law which shall abridge the privileges or immunities of citizens of the United States; nor shall any State deprive any person of life, liberty, or property, without due process of law; nor deny to any person within its jurisdiction the equal protection of the laws.

Page 33: Bill S. 662

Transcription excerpt

Be it enacted by the Senate and House of Representatives of the United States of America in Congress assembled, That the civil government actually existing in Georgia is provisional only, and in all respects subject to the paramount authority of the United States at any time to abolish, modify, control, or supersede the same, until a legislature organized in accordance with the requirements of the act of July nineteenth, eighteen hundred and sixty-seven, shall have duly ratified the amendment to the Constitution of the United States, proposed by the Thirty-ninth Congress, and known as article fourteen, when the State, according to the act aforesaid, ill be subject to the fundamental condition that the constitution of the State shall not be so amended or changed as to deprive any citizen of the United States, or class of citizens, of the right to vote in such State, who are entitled to vote by the constitution thereof herein recognized, except as a punishment for such crimes as are now felonies at common law, whereof they have been duly convicted, under laws equally applicable to all the inhabitants of the State: And provided, That any alteration of the constitution may be made to the time and place of residence of voters.

Page 46: Fifteenth Amendment to the U.S. Constitution

Transcription excerpt

Article XV.
Section 1. The right of citizens of the United States to vote shall not be denied or abridged by the United States or by any State on account of race, color, or previous condition of servitude—
Section 2. The Congress shall have the power to enforce this article by appropriate legislation.

Page 54: Civil Rights Act of 1964

Transcription excerpt

An Act
To enforce the constitutional right to vote, to confer jurisdiction upon the district courts of the United States to provide injunctive relief against discrimination in public accommodations, to authorize the Attorney General to institute suits to protect constitutional rights in public facilities and public education, to extend the Commission on Civil Rights, to prevent discrimination in federally assisted programs, to establish a Commission on Equal Employment Opportunity, and for other purposes.

Be it enacted by the Senate and House of Representatives of the United States of America in Congress assembled, That this Act may be cited as the "Civil Rights Act of 1964".

GLOSSARY

abolitionist A person who opposed slavery.

act A bill signed into law by Congress.

amendment A change made to the Constitution.

amnesty A government pardon granted to one or more people, usually for political offenses.

black codes Rules invented in the South after the Civil War to restrict the rights of blacks.

carpetbagger A Northerner who went to the South after the Civil War for political or financial advantage.

Confederacy The informal name for the Confederate States of America, the Southern states that broke from the Union and formed their own government during the American Civil War.

confiscation The act of the government taking private property.

Congress The body of elected lawmakers in the federal government.

Constitution The body of laws that form the foundation of the United States.

federal government The central authority over the individual states in the United States.

freedman A person who has been freed from slavery.

impeach To bring an accusation against a public official, usually in the hopes of removing that official from office.

inaugural address A ceremonial address given by an newly elected official, especially a U.S. president.

pardon To excuse or forgive.

plantation A large estate or farm on which crops are raised, often by resident workers.

ratify To approve an amendment.

Rebel Another name for a Confederate.

redeemer government A Southern state government that had managed to oust all black representation.

Republican One of the two major political parties during the Reconstruction era, dominant in the North. Also called the Party of Lincoln.

scalawag A white Southerner working for or supporting the federal government during Reconstruction.

secede To withdraw or separate from.

segregation The policy or practice of separating people of different races, classes, or ethnic groups, in schools, housing, and public or commercial facilities, especially as a form of discrimination.

suffrage The right to vote.

Union The Northern states that remained loyal to the federal government and fought against the Confederacy.

veto The power of the president to reject a bill passed by Congress.

FOR MORE INFORMATION

The Civil War Library and Museum
1805 Pine Street
Philadelphia, PA 19103
Web site: http://www.netreach.net/~cwlm

Civil War Library and Research Center
94 Green Street, Room 104
Woodbridge, NJ 07095
(732) 326-1611
Web site: http://www.roberteleecwrt.org/cwlrc.html

Gettysburg National Military Park
97 Taneytown Road
Gettysburg, PA 17325-2804
(717) 334-1124
Web site: http://www.nps.gov/gett

The Museum of the Confederacy
1201 East Clay Street
Richmond, VA 23219
Web site: http://www.moc.org

The National Civil War Museum
1 Lincoln Circle at Reservoir Park
Harrisburg, PA 17103
(717) 260-1861
Web site: http://www.nationalcivilwarmuseum.org

United States Civil War Center
Louisiana State University
Raphael Semmes Drive
Baton Rouge, LA 70803
(225) 578-3151
Web site: http://www.cwc.lsu.edu

Web Sites

Due to the changing nature of Internet links, the Rosen Publishing Group, Inc., has developed an online list of Web sites related to the subject of this book. This site is updated regularly. Please use this link to access the list:

http://www.rosenlinks.com/psah/reco

OR FURTHER READING

King, David C. *Civil War and Reconstruction*. New York: John Wiley & Sons, 2003.

Murphy, Richard W. *The Nation Reunited: War's Aftermath*. Alexandria, VA: Time-Life, 1987.

Peacock, Judith. *Reconstruction: Rebuilding After the Civil War*. Mankato, MN: Bridgestone Books, 2002.

Stanchak, John E. *Civil War*. New York: DK Publishing, 2000.

Ziff, Marsha. *Reconstruction Following the Civil War in American History*. Berkeley Heights, NJ: Enslow Publishers, 1999.

BIBLIOGRAPHY

Bowers, Claude Gernade. *The Tragic Era: The Revolution After Lincoln*. Cambridge, MA: Houghton Mifflin, 1929.

Carter, Hodding. *The Angry Scar: The Story of Reconstruction*. New York: Doubleday and Co., 1959.

"Civil War Reconstruction, Racism, the KKK, and the Confederate 'Lost Cause.'"Teacher Oz's Kingdom of History. Retrieved June 2003 (http://www.teacheroz.com/ reconstruction.htm).

Craven, Avery Odelle. *Reconstruction: The Ending of the Civil War*. New York: Holt, Rinehart and Winston, 1969.

Foner, Eric. *Reconstruction: America's Unfinished Revolution 1863–1877*. New York: Harper & Row Publishers, 1988.

Franklin, John Hope. *Reconstruction, After the Civil War*. Chicago: University of Chicago Press, 1994.

McKitrick, E. L. *Andrew Johnson and Reconstruction*. Chicago: University of Chicago Press, 1960.

Stampp, Kenneth M. *The Era of Reconstruction*. New York: Alfred A. Knopf, 1966.

"Toward Racial Equality: *Harper's Weekly* Reports on Black America, 1857–1874." HarpWeek.com. Retrieved October 2003 (http://blackhistory.harpweek.com/4Reconstruction/ReconLevelOne.htm).

PRIMARY SOURCE IMAGE LIST

Page 5: *Map of the United States of America, Showing the Union and Confederate States.* Created by Theodor Ettling and published by Paris Paniconographie de Gillot in 1861. Housed in the Library of Congress in Washington, D.C.

Page 11: *Surrender of Genl Lee, at Appomattox C.H. Va. April 9th 1865.* Hand-colored lithograph by Currier and Ives, circa 1865. Housed in the Library of Congress.

Page 13: Hand-written page from President Abraham Lincoln's second inaugural address. Dated March 4, 1865. Housed in the Library of Congress.

Page 15 (left): Photograph of Charles Sumner, taken between 1860 and 1875. Housed in the Library of Congress.

Page 15 (right): Photograph of Thaddeus Stevens, taken between 1860 and 1875. Housed in the Library of Congress.

Page 17: *Andrew Johnson Taking the Oath of Office in the Small Parlor of the Kirkwood House [Hotel], Washington.* Created in 1865 for *Frank Leslie's Illustrated Newspaper* and housed in the Library of Congress.

Page 19: Photograph of freedmen gathered by a canal in Richmond, Virginia. Taken in April 1865. Housed in the Library of Congress.

Page 21: *Southern Justice.* Political cartoons from March 23, 1867, issue of *Harper's Weekly.* Illustrations by Thomas Nast.

Page 23: First page from Act of April 9, 1866 (Civil Rights Act). Housed in the National Archives in Washington, D.C.

Page 25: Page from the Fourteenth Amendment to the Constitution. Passed by Congress on June 13, 1866. Housed in the National Archives.

Page 28: Wood engraving of two members of the Ku Klux Klan. Created in 1868. Published in *Harper's Weekly*, December 19, 1868. Housed in the Library of Congress.

Page 29: Illustrations of the riots in Memphis, Tennessee. Published in the May 26, 1866, issue of *Harper's Weekly.* Created by Alfred R. Waud. Housed in the Library of Congress.

Page 32: Etching of General Sherman's march to the sea, created by Ritchie, after an original work by F. O. C. Darley. Housed in the Library of Congress.

Page 33: Cover page of 40th Congress 3rd Session bill S. 662. December 9, 1868. Housed in the Library of Congress.

Page 35: *The First Vote.* Wood engraving by Alfred R. Waud. Published in the November 16, 1867, issue of *Harper's Weekly.* Housed in the Library of Congress.

Page 37: Portrait of Edwin M. Stanton. Photographed between 1860 and 1865. Housed in the Library of Congress.

Page 38: Ticket to the Johnson impeachment trial. April 6, 1868.

Page 41: Wood engraving of Hon. John Willis Menard addressing the House of Representatives, Washington, D.C., in 1869. Published in *Frank Leslie's Illustrated Newspaper*, March 20, 1869. Housed in the Library of Congress.

Page 42: Cartoon of a Carl Schurz as carpetbagger. Wood engraving by Thomas Nast. Originally published in the November 9, 1872, issue of *Harper's Weekly.*

Page 44 (left): Portrait of Francis Lewis Cardozo. Photographed between 1870 and 1880. Housed in the Library of Congress.

Page 44 (right): Portrait of James Orr. Photographed between 1855 and 1865. Housed in the Library of Congress.

Page 46: The Fifteenth Amendment. Passed by Congress on February 26, 1869. Housed in the National Archives.

Page 49: Wood engraving showing Wall Street during the Panic of 1873. Illustration published in the October 11, 1873, issue of *Harper's Weekly*. Housed in the Library of Congress.

Page 51: *In for It.* Political cartoon drawn by Thomas Nast in 1876.

Page 53: *The "Strong" Government 1869-1877—The "Weak" Government 1877-1881.* Two-part color lithograph. Illustrated by James Albert Wales in 1880. Housed in the Library of Congress.

Page 54: The Civil Rights Act of 1964. From the National Archives.

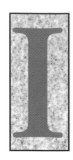

INDEX

B

black codes, 22, 27, 34, 37
Booth, John Wilkes, 16

C

Cardozo, Francis L., 40
carpetbaggers, 41–42, 44, 45
Chamberlain, Daniel Henry, 52
civil rights/equality, 14, 24, 34, 38, 40,
        48, 54
Civil Rights Acts, 24, 35, 54
Civil War, 6, 10, 14, 18, 31, 40, 45, 50, 54
Confederate army, 6, 10, 12, 18, 27, 43
Confederate States of America, 4, 6, 7,
        12, 14, 15, 16, 17, 20, 26, 34, 40,
        52–53
    amnesty program for, 12, 18, 20, 31
Congress, U.S., 6, 7, 12, 14, 15, 16, 18, 20,
        22, 24, 26, 29, 31, 32, 36, 37, 39, 40,
        45, 47, 48, 50

D

Davis, Jefferson, 31
Democratic Party/Democrats, 7, 15, 16,
        22, 26, 37, 50, 51, 52
Democrats, Southern, 16, 20, 22, 30, 37,
        44, 48
Dunn, Oscar J., 39–40

E

Enforcement Act, 47

F

Flournoy, R. W., 43
Fifteenth Amendment, 45–47
Fourteenth Amendment, 24–26, 34,
        35–36, 47, 52, 53
Freedmen's Bureau, 18–19, 22, 24, 37, 42,
        47, 53
Freedmen's Bureau Act, 24

G

Grant, Ulysses S., 10, 28, 36, 38, 47, 48, 50

H

Hayes, Rutherford B., 52

J

Johnson, Andrew, 16–18, 19, 20, 22, 24,
        26, 29, 30, 31, 32
    impeachment of, 36–38

K

Ku Klux Klan (KKK), 27, 29, 47

L

Lee, Robert E., 10
Lincoln, Abraham, 6, 12, 14, 15, 16, 18, 52
Longstreet, James A., 43

M

Menard, John W., 40
Mississippi Plan, 51

O

Orr, James L., 43

P

Panic of 1873, 50
plantation system, 7, 17
planter class, 16, 43

R

racism/racial prejudice, 24, 26, 27–29, 34,
        39, 40, 43, 54
Radical Republicans, 14, 15, 16, 18–19,
        20, 22, 24, 27, 30, 31, 32, 36, 37, 40,
        42, 43, 47, 48
Reconstruction Acts, 32–36, 47
redeemer governments, 45
Republican Party/Republicans, 7, 15, 18,
        22, 26, 30, 31, 32, 43, 45, 47, 48, 50,
        51, 52, 53

S

scalawags, 43, 44

Schurz, Carl, 6–7

segregation, 52

Sherman, William T., 31, 36

slaves/slavery, 4, 6, 7, 10, 12, 16, 32, 39, 40, 43, 52

    education and, 39–40

    equal rights for, 14

    ex-slaves/freedmen, 10, 12, 14, 18, 19, 29, 30, 31, 32, 35, 39, 42, 43

    land grants for, 30–31, 32, 34

Stanton, Edwin M., 31, 36

Stevens, Thaddeus, 14, 24, 30, 31, 34, 40, 43, 48, 53

suffrage, 47

Sumner, Charles, 14, 24, 34, 48, 53

T

Thirteenth Amendment, 12, 53

U

Union, the, 6, 7, 12, 14, 15, 26, 45, 53

Union army, 6, 10, 26, 28, 29, 34, 35, 36

U.S. Constitution, 4, 12, 24, 34

V

vote, right to, 14, 20, 27, 34, 43, 47, 51

W

Whiskey Ring, 50–51

About the Author

Timothy Flanagan holds degrees from the University of California at Berkeley and the University of Iowa. He has published dozens of poems in literary journals and makes his living in the private sector as a business analyst and technical writer. A devoted husband and proud father, Timothy lives with his wife and two sons in Redondo Beach, California.

Photo Credits

Cover, pp. 11, 15, 17, 19, 32, 37, 44, 53 Library of Congress, Prints and Photographs Division; pp. 1, 28, 29, 35, 42, 49 © Corbis; p. 5 Library of Congress, Geography and Map Division; p. 13 Library of Congress, Manuscript Division, The Papers of Abraham Lincoln; pp. 21, 41, 51 © Bettmann/Corbis; pp. 23, 25, 46, 54 National Archives and Records Administration, General Records of the United States Government, Record Group 11; p. 33 Library of Congress, Records of the United States Senate; p. 38 David J. and Janice L. Frent Collection/Corbis.

Designer: Tahara Anderson; **Editor:** Christine Poolos;
Photo Researcher: Peter Tomlinson